The Golden M.....

JOHN GLENDAY's first collection, *The Apple Ghost*,
won a Scottish Arts Council Book Award and his second,
Undark, was a Poetry Book Society Recommendation.
His most recent collection, *Grain* (Picador, 2009),
was also a Poetry Book Society Recommendation and
was shortlisted for both the Ted Hughes Award
and the Griffin International Poetry Prize.

John Glenday

The Golden Mean

PICADOR

First published 2015 by Picador
an imprint of Pan Macmillan
20 New Wharf Road, London N1 9RR
Associated companies throughout the world
www.panmacmillan.com

ISBN 978-1-4472-5391-4

Printed and bound by CPI Group (UK) Ltd, Croydon, CR0 4YY

For Garry, Daniel, Didi, Jack, Matthias
and again, and always, for Erika.

'I know that love is life's best work.'
William Matthews

Contents

The Matchsafe 1

Abaton 2

A Pint of Light 3

Self Portrait in a Dirty Window 4

Primroses 5

Algonquin 6

Allt Dearg 7

Ill Will 8

Fable 9

Two Ravens 10

Song for a Swift 11

Humpback Embryo 12

Mussels in Brine 13

How to Pray 14

The Flight into Egypt 15

Lest We Forget 16

Study for the Hands of an Apostle 17

The Coalfish   18

Blossom Street   19

The Skylark   20

Amber   21

The Ghost Train   22

The Steamer 'Golden City'   24

A Testament   25

The Lost Boy   26

The Big Push   29

Rubble   31

Our Dad   32

The Iraqi Elements   33

The Doldrums   35

The Golden Mean   36

The Grain of Truth   37

Northeasterly   38

Macapabá   39

Only a leaf for a sail   40

Fetch   41

Fetch II 42

The Dockyard 43

Fireweed 44

Monster 45

X Ray 46

The White Stone 47

British Pearls 48

The Constellations 49

Lacerta 50

The Moon is Shrinking 51

Windfall 52

The Darkroom 53

My Mother's Favourite Flower 54

Elegy 55

The Walkers 56

Notes 59

Acknowledgements 61

The Golden Mean

The Matchsafe

for AN

If you must carry fire, carry it in
your heart – somewhere sheltered but hidden,
polished by hands that once loved it.

The lining may be scorched and blackened
but only you must ever know this.
That easy hush you sometimes hear at night

as the darkness stirs in you, is not
the accustomed ache of blood, but a flame
shivering against the wind –

a meagre flame seeded long before you were born
which you have always known must be kept
burning forever, and offered to no one.

Abaton

(from the Greek a, not; baino, I go)

Let's head for a place, neighbouring and impossible,
that city neither of us has ever found;
it swithers somewhere between elsewhere
and here, anchored to the leeward dusk
fettered in cloud.

Look how it flourishes in decline —
no buttresses, no walls, no astragals,
only those luminous avenues of weather
gathering the cluttered light like window glass,
all furnished in the traceries of wind and rain.

A Pint of Light

When I overheard my father say
it was his favourite drink, I closed my eyes
and imagined his body filled with a helpless light.

Years later, I watched him pour out
the disappointing truth, but still couldn't let
that image go: he's trailing home from the pub

singing against the dark, and each step
he steps, each breath he breathes, each note he sings
turns somehow into light and light and light.

Self Portrait in a Dirty Window

after James Morrison, 'The Window 1961'

Don't grumble if this window grants
you only what you see in it.

If you must have light, step out into the world.
If you need shadow, step out into the light.

For once, there is no weight in detail. Who cares
if that's an oily handprint, a belaboured

field or far-off hills? The dirt stain of uncertainty
is all that matters. It fills the room

with neither light nor dark, but the promise
of meaning, which, in itself, means nothing

though it's what you came here for.

Primroses

after Sir William George Gillies

Picked flowers on a rug are dangerous
beyond reason. Their mouths hang

empty of pollen or scent. Such a clamour
of petals, each cut throat challenges

the room, renders it uninhabitable.
A shout, a condemnation, a curse, a denial.

What use is Spring to us now? What purpose
a room charged with such desperate light?

Even as we abandon it, their small voices
will follow us, their bitter faces gape.

Algonquin

for GH and RS

Each dusk is the final dusk. Late mists
forget themselves above the lake.
A crowd of hemlock, shoulder-close and motherly
whispers as its own reflection drowns.
Somewhere not here, a loon calls
out the word for darkness twice,
then turns into the silence and its song.

I kneel where the water frays, and from my hands
build the cracked prayer of a cup.
Let me drink once more; just a little –
one mouthful, one sip would be enough.
Just this time let my hands not leak.
Let them be brimming when I raise them
to my lips, like this.

Allt Dearg

This burn runs dark and sweet
as the lining of the soul.

Drink from me
and you will always be thirsty.

Ill Will

So. First night of the filling moon
I took me to that spoiled oak, skewed
on its fold of hill above my father's farm.

This left hand hefting his pigman's maul
and under my tongue an old King's penny
vague with spending.

Watched while the sparling moon kicked free
from a trawl of cloud, swam on. Then hammered
the penny to its rim in the faulted grain

and wished down the worst on him by three times
wishing it: '*Tree, by your own dead hand,*' says I,
'*wither that blown onion in him no one calls a heart.*'

All the path home the stink of night
in the yarrow and dwarf butterbur. Shriek
of the hen-owl restless in her nothing.

Days passed; something he couldn't rage against
whittled him to a skelf, laid him out hushed
and bloodless; grew him his stone.

All this in the month that wears my name. Meanwhile
I followed ploughshare's hunger through his fields.
Whistled in the old mare's wake. Tasted coin.

Fable

Remember that old tale
of the half-blind angel
fell in love with herself
in a frozen pool?

'Tell me;' she whispers,
'tell me your name,
more smoke of skin
or skein of hair than man.

'Love is the self dissolved.
Lift up to your face
the mirror of my face
and you'll see nothing.'

Two Ravens

for DK and SB

If I were given the choice,
I would become that bird Noah
first sent out to gauge the Flood.

But I would never come back.
I would never come back because
I would find another just like me

and the two of us, casting ourselves
for shadows, would sweep on like a thought
and its answer over depths and shallows

and never rest until the last waves
had unfurled, beating our wings
against the absence of the world.

Song for a Swift

be owl
my oldest night

be wren
my selfish grief

be gull
my restlessness

be lark
my disbelief

be hawk
my hidden path

be dove
my weary fist

be swift
my only soul

my only soul
be swift

Humpback Embryo

Field Collection, South Atlantic Ocean 1949

Big as a dead man's foot, but closer
to tripes or dough than meat.

Just to be sure, they folded her around herself
head-down in formalin. Her one brief sea.

Note that fluke-stump nicked by her mother's
flenser's blade; the flipper's grace.

Day after day, she grows the milk bloom of a thing
that never moved in cold, green, deepening light;

like most of us. The eye-slit weary, delicate,
beyond insult and closed against our looking.

Mussels in Brine

Their ten-a-penny cunts bob in formalin;
the lips slackened, fading to olive drab.

I imagine them weary of being mouthed,
pickled on tedium, flaccid and tired.

They reek of estuary dirt; a tang
of sediment and brackish wine.

Lord, let their valves be opened to me;
let all things preserved be consumed

all but that single grain of sand
gritting between the teeth; flinty, neglected,

enduring as regret, reminding me of you.

How to Pray

If you ever decide you want to find God
look for him in a ploughed field, not high

overhead, in the drift of the distant weather.
And if you ask me how you should pray

to a buried God, I would say press
your lips into the earth, weight your voice

with the silence of earth and root and seed
and pray that all your prayers may be stones.

The Flight into Egypt

after Policarpo de Oliveira Bernardes

Like so much of the Bible, it's predictably domestic:
just a family on its way somewhere, skirting
a thread of towns. Everything is rumours of blue,

because they are in history. No one has courage
enough to look ahead. Joseph glowers
at the chafing calf-boots he bartered for in Bethlehem.

Mary pretends to doze, her fingers locked
around the swaddle. Even their guardian angel
has turned to look back – his know-all smile

encompassing the dusty road, Judaea
diminishing and the almost-new-born who stares
complacently over our right shoulders into today.

Only the old donkey gazes towards Egypt; head down,
ears back, grudging a burden that is worth so little
and a pointless journey he knows has barely begun.

Lest We Forget

Sari Çizmeli Mehmet Aga – Peder Ås – Tommy Atkins – Chichiko Bendeliani – Joe Bloggs – Jane Doe – Jäger Dosenkohl-Haumichblaue – Fulan al-Fulani – Kari Holm – Hong Gildong – Aamajee Gomaajee Kaapse – Kovacs Janos – Janina Kowlaska – Lisa Medel-Svensson – Madame Michu – Jan Modaal – Erika Mustermann – Numerius Negidius – Nguyen Van A – No Nominado – Seán Ó Rudaí – A N Other – Vardenis Pavardenis – Pera Peric – Petar Petrov – Juan Piguave – Ion Popescu – Vasiliy Pupkin – Imya Rek – Mario Rossi – Joe Shmoe – Maria da Silva – Sicrana de Tal – Tauno Tavallinen – Manku Thimma – Jef Van Pijperzete – Wang Wu – Moishe Zugmir

Study for the Hands of an Apostle

after Dürer

This loophole where the light lets in,
and my own breath leaks through my hands,
has damned my words to words or less.

That shim of air is God, of course,
who made us all, and all but whole
then set the wind against the world.

The Coalfish

Pollachius virens

Like a gutting knife lost overboard,
or a tin flag hoisted against the gloom,
or a lime-white flame lit in the heart

of nowhere, the coalfish waits.
He's watching for us. How I wish he had
been named for the perfect

darkness gathered in his eye –
that bead of obsidian set in mother-of-pearl
so perfect it could hold the world.

A tin flag. A white lamp burning
in the founds of the sea.
The gutting knife's quick flame.

Blossom Street

All that awful mess still lies ahead of him of course:
the silly posturing and bombast, those terrifying
stylish uniforms, the sticky end. For the time being

he's sitting by his mother now her illness has finished
its work. The sickroom carpet ankle-deep in his mediocre
sketches of her, endlessly rehearsing every incidence

of light – all those angles and shadows suffering worked
into her, as if somehow one loss might be lost in many
versions of itself. The traffic dims to a respectful hush.

Echoes skitter in the stairwell, then the impatience of a single
knock. Yes. The time has come to put the pencil down.
From this day forward, the only pages will be blank pages.

The Skylark

*'Again and again it would try to hover
over that miniature meadow . . .'*

One square of turf to floor
my cage, one daisy opening,
one little sun against the sky,

one cloud, one thread of wind,
one song to hang
like nothing over everything.

Amber

Some wounds weep precious through the generations.
They glaze and harden, heal themselves into history.

What was mere sap matures like blood in air to darken
and burnish. To change into something useful, almost.

The Tsar had a whole room built from hurt but it was stolen
and buried. Sometimes the grim Baltic rolls the scars

to shape those jewels women love to wear; especially
treasured where they hold a thing that was living once,

something with quick, venated wings which happened
by and thought the wound looked beautiful and sweet

and that, like other wounds, it should be acknowledged
somehow and, if only for a moment, touched.

The Ghost Train

a twinned sonnet

Roy, this is how it finishes: we're riding Dante's Inferno together –
that cheapskate ghost train where Fred Hale hides from his killers

in *Brighton Rock*. I'm Fred, of course, and you're my friendly murderer,
my twin, the one doomed to be sitting alone when the car shudders

to a halt in the din and glare of a South Coast early summer.
This is what life is all about – cheap shocks and clapboard horrors

the whole scene clichéd and overblown – the way the two of us peer
down into the abyss beneath the rails: a seethe of black, impatient water

fretting the stanchions that hold us clear of purgatorial fire.
When you looked into my face, you looked into a mirror,

and smiled, and took my shoulder, held me safe, then pushed me over.
My eyes opened five minutes early, yours closed two decades late.

Is that the tide I hear behind us, or the ghost train's plywood thunder,
or the clutter clutter clutter of loose film clearing the gate?

John, you died two decades early, I was born five minutes late.
Two frames of the one short film – that's really all we were.

Now that one frame is cut, I'll carry back twice the weight –
your life folded in mine – to 1921. We're boys again – back in the foyer

of the Regent with Nanny. Valentino breaks her dusty heart four
times in a single week. We saw it here for the first time – the raw power

of film: that dance! Death galloping from the clouds, the Great War
breaking like a sea against their lives, and in the end, *The End*, a blur

of shadows between fresh graves, the audience all shiftless whispers.
A hundred times we sat in that immense, small dark, and breathed air

rich with smoke and sweat – the reek of a strange, new fire. Remember,
we filed out glazed and dumb with joy and dark – back to the trashy glare

of life going dimly on. John, next time we stumble out into the light together,
guess which of us will blink, and which will disappear?

The Steamer 'Golden City'

after Eadweard Muybridge

Far from the sea, you still feel part of it —
all those dull impatient lights,
that reckless hush. But the way

the morning breaks against itself
marks progress of a sort; like a prow
digging under, ploughing the hours white.

Even on land, even right here at home,
you find yourself stalled by the sense
of something you cannot see dividing

and falling away behind.
And you wish it could be real, that wake
trailing back beyond ocean or purpose;

something to prove to anyone
who cared notice that for a time,
if only a moment, you were going somewhere.

A Testament

I was so young. I wanted to *experience* the world, so I stared at the sun until my eyes burned hollow; kissed all the women I could ever love until each kiss dwindled to water. Now hardly a day passes but I find myself blundering into the sea; or gathering in my arms an unspeakable fire.

The Lost Boy

im Alexander Glenday died November 4th, 1918

November,   and nothing said.
The old world   whittling down
to winter.   Ice on my tongue:
its wordless,   numbing welcome.

We bloody   believed in war
once; we cheered   when our children
sailed off for   the Front. But now
all language   fails me. Listen:

'Army Form   B. 104.
November   1918.'
'...a report   has been received
from the Field, France...   ...was killed in

Action.' There.   Alexander
has been killed –   my couthie boy.
Nineteen, looked   more like fourteen.
They told me   his howitzer

was shattered –   a shell 'cooked off'
in the breech,   and the blast tore
them apart.   They were too keen
of course, boys   blown to pieces

with that Great   War days from won.
Boom. And gone.   I'm a blacksmith.
I've seen what   white hot metal
makes of flesh.   My own wee Eck.

I'm to blame.   I was the fool
who signed, and   him still far too
young. Fifteen!   His mother flung
her mug at   me, mute with rage.

Each morning   she makes his bed;
lays fresh clothes   across a chair.
She'll not speak   his name again.
Her stare is   a hard, black sloe.

If fine rhymes   rang like iron,
hammered bright,   hot with meaning
they might weigh   more in my heart.
Brave songs don't   bring the dead home;

they damn them   to cross that dour
black stream where   yon pale boatman
waits and foul   foundries spit and
silence is   their only song.

When we go   to his grave, I'll
bring sorrel,   because I know
the dead are   always drouthy —
their dry mouths   clotted with dust.

I'll say sorry   son, this plant
slakes only   the one, small thirst;
may its brief   white blossom
linger upon   your grave, like snow.

The Big Push

after Sir Herbert James Gunn, 'The Eve of the Battle of the Somme'

Would you believe it, there's a bloke out there singing
'When You Come to the End of a Perfect Day'.
His audience, a sixty-pounder crew, stand round bleeding
from the ears. The Boche are all but finished, apparently –

I heard they're packing old clock parts into trench mortars
now, for want of iron scrap. Some wag quips that next time he's
sentry and hears the plop of a *minenwerfer* tumbling over,
he'll not blow the alarm, he'll shout: *'Time, gentlemen, please . . .'*

We laugh and for one heartbeat forget to be afraid. Bravery
and cowardice are just two workings of the same fear
moving us in different ways. The 8th East Surreys
have been given footballs to kick and follow at Zero Hour;

it's to persuade them from the trenches lest their nerve fail
as they advance on Montaubon. I've watched men
hitch up their collars and trudge forward as if shrapnel
and lead were no worse than a shower of winter rain.

This afternoon a few of us went swimming in the mill dam
behind Camp. Just for a while to have no weight, to go drifting
clear of thought and world, was utter bliss. A skylark climbed
high over the torn fields on its impossible thread of song:

'*like an unbodied joy.*' I don't know why, but it reminded
me of the day we took over from the French along the Somme;
it was so tranquil, so picturesque, the German trenchworks crowded
with swathes of tiny, brilliant flowers none of us could name.

I believe if the dead come back at all they'll come back green
to grow from the broken earth and drink the gathered water
and all the things they suffered will mean no more to them
than the setting-in of the ordinary dark, or a change of weather.

Rubble

General term for a people who are harvested and reused
or broken. To be heaped randomly or roughly stored.
That which is held for common use. Infill. Of little worth.

Break them in different ways but they will always be the same.
Hold them in the dark; remind yourself why they should stay forgotten.
These days there is little interest in stones that bear names.

May they be piled up and given this title in common.
Let them take their place in the register of unspoken things.
May they never be acknowledged again.

Our Dad

After he'd passed over, she buried all his séance books.
Said she was comfortable with the notion of the Afterlife
but had no use for it on her parlour shelf. It felt worse
than burning somehow – imagine words gasping for air,

their loosened pages mouldering back to soil and dirt.
In the thirties, he was a regular at Circle meetings in some
North London suburb, but didn't believe in an afterlife
or the Spirit Realm, that sunlit somewhere after death.

It was the showmanship he loved: all that cheerless
determination, cotton wool and wire; all that nifty
fiddling with lights. Let death be always nothing more
than sleight of hand. One flurry of white doves

and the earth-strewn dead spring back into our lives,
gaping and astonished. Cue the applause. Amen to that.

The Iraqi Elements

after Zaher Mousa

This is the birth of Water:
Mist is when water dies so that it can be born again.
Sluggish rivers swither among the dead,
their banks overflowing.
Listen: those whisperings in the pipework
are all the refugees from thirst.
The inscription on the fountain's cup reads:
'Drink, Hussain, and remember thirst.'
Their fathers: their fathers' gentle thirst,
like sand slowly pouring into blood;
heedless as a stone: a millstone that worries
its own reflection back to sand.
So they went off to war and when they came back,
no water for the ritual cleansing,
not one drop, so they washed themselves in graveyard dust.

*****

This is the birth of Air:
Weary angels revel in it: the sky is laced
with the gutturals of genies; those dark eyes
that glimpse the invisible smouldering in their veins.
Here you touch against breasts that breathed in childhood's loss.
Their women: their women are perfumed sadnesses;

their gaze carried away on the wind
bleached of all colour: their black clothes
abandoned – still in suitcases somewhere.
The women banked on hard graft and the smoking *tanur*,
but War won that bet, of course. War always does.
And when it was all over they breathed in the soot of a crow's wing;
the drift of fans through narrow rooms.

*****

This is the birth of Fire:
Soldiers trudge home from the front line.
Slivers of shrapnel glimmer inside them.
Here's a dead man with a cigarette in his pocket,
still alight – his last smoke.
Cancers flare and smoulder in the heads of children.
Their children: their children with happiness chalked into their faces –
if they were a pack of cards there wouldn't be any joker.
Their children are little crusts of bread dunked
in muddy kerbside puddles. Life will gobble them up.
In other countries children have footballs to play with, but not here,
no, in this country they used the children's heads as footballs.

*****

This is the birth of Earth: Feel this: feel the earth.

The Doldrums

after Zaher Mousa

I

I'll carry this wound like a wristwatch – look
it's bleeding the minutes away;
but leaves no mark, no scar on Time
though day wears day down into day.

II

Dear afternoon,
I only glimpsed you as you sailed past my window
and vanished forever, like that girl on the bus,
that hopelessly beautiful girl.

III

No. My blood is nothing like the honest river
glazing and slackening through the seasons.
Think of a worn-out wall-clock with its dodgy weathers:
faster and faster, then slower again, then . . .

The Golden Mean

I am to you
as you are
to us and

we are to
everything.

The Grain of Truth

Grows poorly in rich soil. Ripening
demands an exceptional season.

Blights more readily than us, even.
Sow it, you'll reap a fine harvest of sorrow.

Each head clings grimly to husk and chaff,
mills the stoutest millstone

to a gritty pebble, kills all yeasts,
sulks in the oven like its own headstone.

So never offer me something
I cannot refuse and expect thanks.

Don't bring me this gift then
ask me why I cannot thrive.

Northeasterly

Driven by sleet and hail,
snell, dour and winterly;

it fills the unwilling sail,
empties the late, green tree.

Something unknowable
lodged in the heart of me

empties itself and fills
Like that sail. Like that tree.

Macapabá

We rocked at anchor where the emptying
river spreads its green hand.
Ochre mud thickened the sea.

On the second morning, slender boats
from the forest; they brought birds
the colour of watered oil,

sallow fruit no one would taste
and a leaf folded around a knot of gold
broader than a clenching fist.

Only a leaf for a sail

and before us, look, the impossible ocean of it all;

squall and storm;

      lash and flail;

the unnavigable, the hungry, the whole perfect

unstarred bleakness of the world,

as though a dark

we had always feared had grown real and cold and tidal,

and the lifted

green-black

ragged face of its hand to pull us,

             pull us down,

and what chance would you say we had,

                 so small,

only the two, my love, just me,

        just you,

but give us a leaf for a sail, and suddenly, somehow,

everywhere's possible.

Fetch

Now that she is lost to us. Now that
she has come back, restless.

Now that we no longer believe in her,
let her ribcage crumble

with the bricks in the old warehouse
that almost remembers;

let her breath smell of iron scab,
of diesel, of lime;

let her skin be the bloom
on oily setts, let her voice

be loose sections of fencework
shivering in the wind.

Let her call out through last night's dark
towards today. Let her not be heard.

Fetch II

She's so real you can hardly see her, printed
like Christ's face into cloth; the linen
rehearsing his wounds while they rusted in the air.

Her eyes turn from the empty warehouse
to the winking lights on the dock, the salt-dark firth
and the far hills brewing cumuli.

Don't be sad, she says, *Don't grieve for any of this.*
(her footsteps sweetening back to dust)
This sort of emptiness could save us all.

The Dockyard

Buddleia does well here, at least.
It thrives on flowers of sulphur, concrete dust,
coiled swarf and radon's heavy bloom.

No wonder the petals gleam the utter blue
of a welder's flame. No wonder the blossom
rusts so easily, a shiver in the grass-choked guttering.

In summer, butterflies briefly linger here,
all the colours of ash and earth and blood.
See how they diminish towards cloud and light

as their fragile clockwork unwinds through
the onshore wind, high over the dual carriageway
and corner shops, towards the hills.

Fireweed

I'm old enough to remember how dangerous
they were, those steam trains butting the weather
south of Forfar, heading for the big smoke.

They would seed sparks among the dropped coals littering
the ballast by the Seven Arches, sweetening the shale for weeds.
Even as we speak the willowherb is hitching upwind

through the decades; it feeds on old burnings,
hungry for nitrogen. At Doig's Farm, their purple heads
crowd above watermint and nettle, or lean out over

the slackwater pools to marvel at themselves – tall, aristocratic,
raised out of last year's waste, abandonment and fire.

Monster

'I have no doubt of seeing the animal today . . .'

I miss it all so much – family and everything.
Father in that lab coat fathers wear;
always too close, always too distant,

always too keen. You may have heard –
my mother was the product of unmentionable
absences and storms; my siblings

a catalogue of slack, discarded failures.
We are all born adult and unwise;
don't judge me too harshly.

Which of us was not cobbled into life
by love's uncertain weathers? Are we not
all stitched together and scarred?

Step forward any one of you who can say
they are not a thing of parts.

X Ray

The grinning moon lies
balanced on a haze of cloud,
snagged in the thousand

branches of a bare
white tree. But these
are nothing – nothing's marks,

pauses for thought,
the interstices, the points
at which something slowed

and thickened as it made
its way through her. Surely
this speaks of a wilful

hesitancy – interest even?
For want of the proper science
we should call that love.

The White Stone

when you take it
in your hand

it will weigh smooth
and hard and cold

as the heart once did
long ago

before it was first
touched by the world

British Pearls

'Gignit et Oceanus margarita, sed subfusca ac liventia . . .'
(Tacitus Agricola 1:12)

British pearls are exceptionally poor.
They can be gathered up by the handful wherever
surf breaks, but you'll find no colour, no vitality, no lustre
to them – every last one stained the roughshod grey
of their drab and miserable weather.

Imagine all the rains of this island held
in one sad, small, turbulent world.
I can hear them falling as I write. British pearls
are commonplace and waterish and dull,
but their women wear them as if winter were a jewel.

The Constellations

The trick is always to appear fixed,
whatever happens. To hold the pattern

we were born to, though its significance
may be lost to us. Here is where we make

our stand and our love will be defined not by
touch or glance but by the distances

mapped out between us. We'll light
everything that needs our light, steadfast

as the stars we fell from, trusting
in them through disaster and adversity,

though we know in our hearts
they are burning in their shackles, like us all.

Lacerta

Not the browbeaten old king,
or his poor wife handcuffed to her capsized throne,

or their sad and lonely daughter
waiting in the darkness for her perfect monster.

Not the dead swan nailed to its right ascension
or those pointless feathers harnessed to a stallion.

Grant me the bleakness of the northern sky
and a yellow gaze that burns relentlessly

and the scales and the claws and the flickering tongue
of a constellation none of you can name.

The Moon is Shrinking

It isn't just at night the moon sheds its skin. All day
you can watch white dust catch the light as it settles
on the world, turning distance the watery blue of faded
colour photographs. How long can this go on?
Each year the moon grows lighter while we grow heavier.
Can you not feel it as you walk the streets, how gravity deepens
and there always appears to be more to us than we know there is?
Each new step more arduous. Have you not noticed
how year by year the tides abandon us? Each month
the blood less eager to flow; each month the pain more distant,
more unreal. The day might come when you will forget
your suffering, and reach out to it.

Windfall

What is love if it is not an unravelling
against the dark? In the moonless field
between house and river, remember

how you stood with your arms
wide to the night, under every tumid
star, waiting for one to drop.

The Darkroom

im WK

If I am the one who is said to be
alive, and you the other, how come it's me
who ends up trailing along behind

as you stride ahead, humming
to yourself, crossing from shade to shadow?
Every morning I wake

longing for you to long for me again;
to dawdle, to loiter, and then – to hell
with the cost, I say – look back.

My Mother's Favourite Flower

This world is nothing much – it's mostly
threadworn, tawdry stuff, of next to little use.

If only it could bring itself to give us back
a portion of the things we would have fallen

for, but always too busy living, overlooked
and missed. So many small things missed.

So many brief, important things.
It is my intention never to write about this.

Elegy

and now that
his song is done

open your hands
there can be no

harm in that
let the notes go free

let them become
ash in the wind

gone back
not to nothing

no
to everything

The Walkers

As soon as we had died, we decided to walk home.
A white tatterflag marked where each journey began.
It was a slow business, so much water to be crossed,
so many dirt roads followed. We walked together but alone.

You must understand – we can never be passengers any more.
Even the smallest children had to make their own way
to their graves, through acres and acres of sunflowers
somehow no longer pretty. A soldier cradled a cigarette, a teddy bear

and his gun. He didn't see us pass, our light was far too thin.
We skirted villages and cities, traced the meanderings of rivers.
But beyond it all, the voices of our loved ones called
so we flowed through borders like the wind through railings

and when impassable mountains marked the way,
soared above their peaks like flocks of cloud, like shoals of rain.
In time the fields and woods grew weary and the sea began –
you could tell we were home by the way our shadows leaned.

We gathered like craneflies in the windowlight of familiar rooms,
grieving for all the things we could never hold again.
Forgive us for coming back. We didn't travel all this way
to break your hearts. We came to ask if you might heal the world.

Notes

Abaton: '. . . a town of changing location. Though not inaccessible, no one has ever reached it . . .' – *The Dictionary of Imaginary Places* by Alberto Manguel and Gianni Guadalupi.

The Skylark – the epigraph is taken from the autobiography of John Muir.

The Ghost Train – loosely based on the lives of the filmmakers John and Roy Boulting.

The Lost Boy – The poem is based on Sonatorrek (Loss of Sons) from Egil's saga and is written in the Viking ballad-metre '*kviðuháttr*'.

The Iraqi Elements – tanur – a wood-fired oven.

Monster – the epigraph is taken from a letter written by Mary Wollstonecraft to her husband on August 30th, 1797, the day Mary Shelley was born.

ACKNOWLEDGEMENTS

Individual poems have appeared in the following publications:

13 Magazine, BODY, Earthlines, Entanglements, The Lampeter Review, The New Edinburgh Review, Gutter, Heavenly Bodies, Ploughshares, The Spectator, Atlanta Review, Irish Pages, Northwords Now, Transnational Literature.

Several poems were first published in collaboration with the photographer Alastair Cook in *Everything We Have Ever Missed*.

'A Pint of Light' was published by Bradford on Avon Arts Festival.

'Self Portrait in a Dirty Window' and 'Primroses' were commissioned for the The Hunterian Gallery, Glasgow.

'The Flight into Egypt' was commissioned for the Felix Festival, Antwerp.

'The Skylark' was originally published as a postcard poem by Alastair Cook.

'The Ghost Train' was commissioned for the anthology *Double Bill*.

'The Lost Boy' was commissioned by the Department of Anglo-Saxon, Norse and Celtic at the University of Cambridge for Modern Poets on Viking Poetry and subsequently produced as a filmpoem by Alastair Cook.

'The Big Push' was commissioned by the Fleming Gallery, London and subsequently produced as an animated film.

'Our Dad' was commissioned by Kevin Reid for his anthology *The Lord's Prayer*.

'The Iraqi Elements' and 'The Doldrums' were translated during translations workshops in Shaqlawa, Iraq, as part of the Reel Iraq 2013 initiative. Many thanks to Lauren Pyott for writing the bridge translations.

'Only a leaf for a sail' was originally published online in '7 Sails'.

'The Walkers' was commissioned by the Dutch filmmaker Judith Dekker.